# Small Town Chase

## Nick Power

*erbacce-press*
**Liverpool UK**

erbacce-press publications Liverpool UK 2013

erbacce-press.com
ISBN: 978-1-907878-61-9

**About the Author:**

Nick Power wrote the brunt of this book whilst waiting around for something else to happen. It is a short chronicle of life growing up in a small town in the north of England, and is almost all lies.

The author wishes to state that any reference to people or place names herein is purely coincidental.

This is his first publication.

*Who could disown*
*themselves now?*

# Contents

## New Animal

I think I'd like
to go back home
for a while

an' just be invisible
you know?

use the microwave a bit

slingshot Crows on telephone
wires

confuse
marine biologists
by planting Starfish
in the surf

ride shotgun
with Chrissy Sparks
and his Great Dane,
its long tongue
hanging
out the back
window
like a big
blue
streamer

wander round supermarkets

maybe watch a B-movie

dawdle across sand dunes

give myself a good
strong dose of
cabin fever

an' come out the
other end
with a new animal
inside me

### Days on my Own

days on
my own

days like this

gold dust
days

rockinghorseshit
days

richesofthepoor
days

rare
days

so rare
I almost don't
know what
to do
with them

and that's
the way
I like
it

## Kings of the Dark
(based on Federico Garcia Lorca's 'Fable
of Three Friends to Be Sung in Rounds')


Carl
Doddy
Lias

you're bound together
by the loose seams
of the night

chain-ganged by
the lost
art of friendship

lolling over
the concrete tongue
of the Wigwam Cathedral
in the drowsy
evening
heat,
you are
golden.

Doddy
Lias
Carl

wake up:
the sun is setting
the third rail is crackling
the chinese supermarkets
are locking up their ghosts

chip papers are singing
you a worksong

Lias
Carl
Doddy,

on their way down
Hardman Street,
the three of them

blue-eyed each
pour petrol on their
palms,
cough rocket fuel
and hooch
from young lungs
cats,
cadavers,
Christ The Redeemer
is listening

three
and two
and one
at the Philharmonic pub
three day hungry,
ski-masked,
point a stolen
pheasant gun
into the
turkeynecked bartenders
gut

(**BANG!**)

three
kings
of the dark
run pocketspewing
with crumpled notes
into the humid
black
Carl with trembling knees
Doddy dead-eyed
Lias smiling
following the neon
to Hackens Hey
and a getaway

watch them
pirouette
over vandalgreased
walls,

wrench their guts
across
railway tracks
watch them stare
head-on
at desperation
and stab
it
through its
red heart

Carl
Doddy
Lias

your bond
was broken
with the loose
seams of the night

Lias staring out
to the black river
from the bars
of Cheapside
bridewell

Doddy
at the Mystery
holding his brain up
to a laughing
moon

Carl
lobotomised,
bull-barred
across the pavement
by a white Mariah

stone dead

birdfeed
for dockyard
scavengers

# Breaking Reds

from the
cracked
lookinglass
of a top floor
window,
a line is
cast
into the
soft
and salted
night

three
flashes
of bright
torchlight-
that whisper
'we're
   ready'-
a trawlernet
loaded with
herringbait,
plunged into
a heaving
sea

and then
the response-
bloodflooded
engines
splutter into
life
in faraway
valley towns
and dewsilk
lined
terraces

the puzzled
voice
of a stolen
ambulance
galloping
down a
dual carriageway,
three motorbikes
at separate
intersections
breaking reds
for
a
razor thin
advantage

then-
the strained
duffelbag
is dropped
ten storeys,
kissing
the kerbside
quiet
as a tablecloth,
coaxing
the needy
and the greedy
into
the hot tarpit,
light rain
falling past
dull
streetlamps
like
silver
dancing coins

## White Whale

your mouth
is moving

but the words
are muffled

your eyebrows
are like jumping beans

but your face
is blurred

last night I
dreamed
of a white whale

and there's a
white whale
on your
window-sill

the palm of
your hand
clips my brow

hair and nails
coming towards
me

and I'm thinking
'the sea
is pulling me in
again'

**Christopher Lee**

five o'clock bed
there's a raging river
inside of my head

hula-ka-hula-ka-hula-ka-hum

Christopher Lee
in a burnt out
Capri

lakka lakka wuh wuh ummmmmmmmmmm

a train
a train
at the back of
my brain

schhhhhcum-chcum- schcum-chcum

Benny had an acid
in the Victorian
school

e-war-woo-war-e-war-woo-war

scratched out
his eyes

in the empty
swimming pool

whom baba lu ba a whom bam bu

hey Mr Rain
wont you follow me
down?

Hmmmmmmmmmmmmmmmmmmmm

down to where
the buses
don't run

eee-babu-babu eee-babu-babu

me and you
have some
talking to do

ooma-ga a uma-ga ooma-ga a uma-ga

an' moonlit cornfields
to wander
through

ZZZZzzzzzzzzzzzzzzzzzzzzzzzzzzzzzzzzz

**Small Town Chase**

Chasing the day,
        chasing the night
    and everything inbetween

Chasing skirt,
        Dragons
    n' plumes of purple
            smoke

Music
        dribbling down
    from rotten
        woodliced
            window panes

Chasing God in a comic

A voice in the mattress

Doghair breakfasts in
        wormhole cafe's

Chasing songs from
        the radio
            around a room
            cha-choom-cha-cha-chaaaaaa-chooooom

Chasing desire
        to catch up with it
        and say
            'hold your horses'

Stalactite breath
        on a cold highway
            chasing the moon

Cars passing through
        from one end of town
            to the other

Chasing themselves

Dog chases,
    Horse races

Christmas day in the
    bookmakers

n' wishing you'd won
just one bet
in your whole time
on earth

    'Imagine there's this
        big cinema screen in heaven
      where you get to see
        your life back
         from start to finish'

'I wouldn't watch it if
    they *paid* me'

Chasing that first feeling

of loneliness

of x-ray vision in a dream

Sex

Fantasizing
    about

    Your life and
        mine,
      how it could have been

Chasing that,
      and everything
    in between.

## Morgan's Head

Morgan's head
  is a peat bog

      is a marsh, alive with
          mayonnaise, Sneaky Pete
          Relish

      and Mexican Bandido
          black curly
          hair

      Krayola cartoon
          down
          his chin

Morgan's head
  is a chupacabra

      a three-egg omelette
          in a promenade cafe,
          charred

              a flying saucer
              in a coal shed
              is
                  Morgan's head

Morgans head,
    carjacked by wheezing
        shoulders,
            pole-axed by a
                wooden stake,
                    pearl marble
                        and weeping sore,
                            wobbles

Morgan's head
    says
        'I done this'
    and
        'I done that'
    and
        'I know him'

and

'From Calcutta to Wales I planted a
birch tree in every sewer'

Morgan's head
was embalmed by Egyptians.

Were you there
when Morgan's head
span full circle
in the healing tent?

Did you hear his bones moan
and his fingertips cook?

They laid it down on
a Burlap Bed

Morgan's head.

Morgan's head
took LSD
from a scientist
who lived upstairs

and his Polish girlfriend
wrote down
every word he said

'godgoldwishingwellvitaminacountdownican
timdrowninginthecarpetsnakesinruudgullitsd
readlockwallpaperswirlingnoonebutmymum
everknewsoupharrierjumpjetloveturntheligh
tsoffloveloveloveimwatchingmyselfdie'

when his blue blooded gums
had rotted and bled
she buried it up to
its eyes
when its ears were
dead

Morgan's head

## Do The Gooseneck

when you're
'round here
an' you wanna
blend in

do
The Gooseneck

shake your gills

open up your third eye

wrench them fillings
from your
backteeth

lash them onto
the bar,
say

'four of the same'

an' suddenly
everyone's epileptic

everyone's giving
head,

everyone's summoning
through their
shoelaces,

everyone's doing
The Gooseneck

### Train Hop

you're hopping
from
foot to foot,
making
imaginary moves
on the
paving stone
chessboard

earlier-
we were caught
without a
ticket
on the train
and each had
to pay
a twenty pound
penalty fare

the night had
a momentary
heart attack

but we didn't care-

we left the
body
at the
scene

# Blackout

dogs barking
from empty driveways
  in the
    blackout

a thousand
overheated T.V's
submit
  to the
    blackout

dominoes
semi-final
abandoned
  in the
    blackout

ghosts
discarding
milk-white sheets
  to the
    blackout

two bodies
dragged from
a flooded quarry
  in the
    blackout

seventy-seven
senior citizens
stranded on stairlifts
  in the
    blackout

child killer
crawls from
the sewer
  in the
    blackout

in the Indian restaurant,
every member

of the male voice choir
  sing to the
    blackout

cement mixers
provide entry
to other dimensions
  in a
    blackout

local electricians
sweat into buckets
  through the
    blackout

Jesus Christ
returns briefly
  for the
    blackout

former Miss
    World
see's the mirror crack
  in the
    blackout

Midnight Mass
say ten Hail
Mary's
  in the
    blackout

Rosa-lee
reads the news
upside-down
  in the
    blackout

Time
is a frozen
pendulum
and everyone is blind
  through the
    blackout

# Bear Pit

from the
stem of my
umbrella,

I heard
a voice

a deep
phlegm
gullett-purge
that sounded
like the
deadlydeep
mud
on the banks
of the
Nile,
the new-caldera
forming over
a volcano,
splurging and
bubbling and
farting its way
over
deep craters,
the sound of
wet leaves,
leeches,
scales, fins
and halfbreeds
searching
for
breath
at the top
of rainforest
treetrunks-

a Malamute gnawing
at the
bones

of a businessman
at the bottom
of a
Biffa bin

but nevertheless

a voice

'Go to Eastham Ferry'

I resisted

'Go to Eastham Ferry'

I could hear drums

drums that presaged murder

a ritual
at least

'Go to Eastham Ferry'

the next time I
drag my eyes away
from the pale
sun
I'm staring down
into the old
bearpit
at the derelict
woodlands zoo,
fingernails black
with blood
and a drunk desire
to crawl down there
and sleep,

sleep through the
long winter

## Bull-Spirit

my skin
is hot
to touch-

it's good
to feel
the sun again

drink up the
smell
of new-mown
grass

watch cattle
dawdle
across iron
grids

then wait like
bowling pins
for the great
Bull-Spirit
to charge down
from heaven

and give them
back
their brains

### Reason to Live

Reason to live

A reason to live

Give me one

He demands

Ashen faced,
staring through
tears
at the tiled
hospital floor.

I'm brushing
hair
out of his
eyes

'there's a dog
at home
who
wants feeding'

I say

He begins to tuck
his shirt in

## White Cob

There are two things
I want from
tomorrow

the first is an end
to this heatwave

the second is for
her,
asleep next to me

for her to
start loving me
again

not the run of
the mill
Scott and Charlene
soap opera
love-

I'm talking the
black and white
Hollywood
Gone with the Wind
Clark Gable
love
that she used to
have

where she couldn't
eat or sleep
or laugh
unless she was
with me

which admittedly,
would annoy
me sometimes,

suffocate me
a little

my mind would
constantly drift off

I'd imagine myself on endless
train journeys across
Siberia
or some other place
I'd never been to

with no desire to
love or be loved.

But now that it's gone-

I'd do anything to have
that love back

anything

I'd kill a Swan if I
had to

yes

I could do that without
blinking

if God spoke to me from the
heavens and asked me to
sacrifice a swan
in return
for a single wish,

I'd take it-

I'd drop a huge rock
on the head of a
White Cob,
one foot on its
long, graceful neck

wings flapping

*POP*

Three. a.m.

this is the time I hurt
the most

staring up at cobwebs

the outline of a
giant Aardvark
in a ceiling silhouette

she comes in close to my
shoulder

then pulls away again

### Rescue

Holy King Kong
in the Moonless night
    Rescue me, Rescue me, Rescue me
and the Lucha Libre
wrestlers
on the empty building site
    Rescue me, Rescue me, Rescue me
all blackgummed
sailors,
strangers,
council-tax evaders
space raiders,
bigbreasted women
in bright purple
blazers
    Rescue me, Rescue me, Rescue me
Pterodactyl,
Tibetan Mastiff,
residents of
Jamaica House
and anyone who's
ever thrown
a wobbler,

come out from your
hiding places

onto this
murder mile

guns blazing,

mob-handed,

open-armed,

crying-
ready and willing

to
    Rescue me

## Ulysses

I'll spend years
on it

up in the attic

ignoring her and him and
her and him

burrowing down into
my own thing

bathing my head in buttermilk

Swarfega around my
hands

I'll write a page a
day
like Hemingway

grow a beard

put riddles in the subtext
that only I
know the answers to

that solve the
mystery of Chris Kenny,

Springheel Jack,

The Burbo gypsies

and the gas tunnels underneath
New Brighton baths.

I'll stay up for days on end
till I finish

wired

and people will come up to me
years later
in supermarkets
and chip shop queues
and comic conventions

and say

'How did you write it?'

and I'll hand 'em this poem

## Hula

She hula-hooped
on her front lawn
all day
every Saturday
round and
round and
round
hips moving
in this big yellow
t-shirt
while her father
practised his
putting technique
on the newly
mown
grass

I could always
see them,
just across the
road from my
shabby house,
half painted in pink,
scaffold collapsing
onto the
driveway

round and
round
and round

every Saturday

once,
at the end of a
particularly bad month

I stood outside
with a pile
of rocks at my
feet

'Fore!!!'

I shouted at the
old man

and he looked
up from
his putting position

'FORE!!!'

I shouted again
and hurled the
biggest rock
I had

it missed both
of them
and went straight
through the back
window
of his Ford Estate

car alarm
squealing

I threw a few more
as they ran into
their porch,
this big green hula-hoop
rolling down the
driveway
and straight onto
the pile of junk
that had been
growing on my
lawn

needless to say,
it remains there
to this day

## Christmas Eve

'You owe it to
the boys'

my dad,
red-nosed,
beer-breathed,
stood in the hall,
overcoated
facing his wife

an ongoing
battle
between
head, hands
and zip

ordered back
out
into the night
to pluck a
midnight
Christmas-tree
from a
sleeping lumber
yard
in a force-ten
gale

we stay silent

he glances at us
as he heads
for
the door

our secret
appointment
has been
made

## Robbie

Robbie told me
he'd seen a
snuff movie

which wasn't an
unusual
thing
for Robbie
to say

he was full of
stories
like this one-

endless yarns of
mystery and violence
and out of body
experiences

you probably knew
someone
like Robbie
once

he'd stay
in bed for
days at a
time,
listened to
Bessie Smith
on repeat,
was borderline

alcoholic,
and liked to
talk about his
Scottish
heritage

among other
things.

His favourite
film
was
'Frankenhooker'

"Where'd you see it?"

I prompted him

"The Snuff?"

"Yeah"

"I was at the top
of this tower
block in
Wigan and
someone had
this grainy
videotape.
It was this fella
in a black
balaclava

doing some
bird from behind
with a shotgun.
They're on this
horrible old
shagpile rug.

Anyway, just
as she's about
to come, BLAM!
he pulls
the trigger
and blasts her
stomach all
over the room.
It's supposed to
be the biggest
turn on for
women"

"Shagpile rugs?"
I say
into a bag
of crisps

"No, getting it with
a shotgun you
divvie"

"Oh. I thought
you meant
shagpile rugs"

## On Entering Birkenhead Park
## on a Cold November's Evening

'Bonfire
   funeral pyre
      Sally lie down
         with the guy'

seven girls
of no more than
fourteen years
hand in hand
circling a
scrapheap
fire.

Every so often,
one breaks
the chain
to edge
closer
to the inferno,
to limbo
under the
cinders
and smoke

to test
her will
against the
searing
heat

to get a
closer
look.

'Bonfire,
   funeral pyre,
      Emily light up
         with the guy'

faster now
they spin,
voices hysterical,
white school

socks
and pumps
pounding the
soil,
the pumpkin
orange glow
and crackle
of wood,
round
and
round
and
round

'Bonfire,
    funeral pyre,
        Natalie burn
            with the guy'

its crescendo
is reached
when, unable
to move any
faster,
Natalie, pigtailed
and pinnied,
breaks the chain
and leaps
a supernatural
leap
high into the
furnace,
the charred logs,
the melting
pramwheels,
the toxic smoke
and smell
of cooking
hair,
Natalie bids
us farewell
to go
and sleep
with the
burning man.

## Weekend Away

Things actually work
in Germany

it's great

two minutes
ago
I was feeling thirsty,
so
I walked to a vending
machine,
picked a drink,
put money in,
and the drink
CAME OUT

now, I'm DRINKING IT

it even THANKED ME

now I'm waiting for a train
and I'm able to
*breathe*

they're even saying it'll be
here on time

right now,

British Rail
seems like one of those
dreams you have
when your
ill with the flu-

a distorted face
whizzes by
on a carousel,

somebody whispers
your name
in a faraway cornfield
and you wake up
in pools of sweat,

realise you haven't
seen your mother in a while

then make up a reason
        to go and visit.

## Heal Myself

Heal myself
Heal myself
body
and brain
to
Heal myself

Vinegar and
brown paper
to
Heal myself

Staring long
at
oil rigs
to
Heal myself

Back to the
old house
to
Heal myself

Honey
and the
horsewhip
to
Heal myself

Black
baubles
round the
fireplace
to
Heal myself

A polaroid
bonfire
to
Heal myself

Coughing up
the
cockroach
map
to
Heal myself

An
Indian Rope
trick
to
Heal myself

Lost art of
invisibility
to
Heal myself

Pretending
to be
someone
being
no-one
to
Heal myself

Un-doing
a promise
knot
to
Heal myself

Stealing
croweggointment
to
Heal myself

Hair of
the
dog
to
Heal myself

## The Thing I Remember Most

That day-
we watched a lunar eclipse,
saw two F-15's loop the loop
above a carnival
and saw the blurred faces
of ghosts
whiz round on the
swing-o-rama

But the thing I remember most
is the two braids
in the back of your hair

That night-
we watched the train de-rail
not twelve yards from the platform,
saw two gypsies climb a signal post
for a sparrowhawk egg,
watched snow fall like
fish food onto the
frozen tracks

But the thing I remember most
is the felt-tip tattoo
around your ring finger

The next morning-
we hung onto the darkness
till breakfast television,
drew a map from the Burrito bar, to the
crazy golf, to the Art Gallery, all the way
down Halkyn Avenue.

We watched a river of mud and blood
wash through Australia.

But the thing I remember most
is whistling our way down
to the all-night garage
only to find it shut

That evening-
a tiny earthquake
tiptoed in from the Irish Sea
we watched a martial arts movie
with the sound off
and two Liver Birds swooped down
from their perch
and ripped the hapless
heads off Mr and Mrs Mayor
at the City Hall

But the thing I remember most
is the reflection
of your red hair
in the river,
a dirty, muddy
landslide of a Mersey
now glazed with
a beautiful
blood red rust
swimming all the way
from the Runcorn bridge
down to
Woodchurch ferry

**Elevated Train**

Elevated train,
you buried the world
with your brown fingers

Gave us a date for
Doomsday
on the back of an old ticket
then accelerated away

Elevated train, you're a hearse

You're a Mongol rider dancing
across an iron trestle

Past the moon, past the quarry,
the dull blinking city, past the all
night cafe's, cheapside, the gay
bars and the banks, past a
spewing grain warehouse with
rivulets of bile in its gullet, past our
beautiful cathedral.

Elevated train, you've been hot-
wired

You're a runaway

You were never there, were you?
When we stole the mannequin
from Marksies

to shoot pellets at

We had to abandon it in a
scrapyard skip
because of your no-show

Elevated train, why did you leave
us?

And that lady with the half frozen
face
chasing us onto the platform,
stiletto's scraping on the gravel
steps
lipstick smeared onto her
exposed teeth

She knew all about you

Elevated train, you wake us from
our slumber
You rattle our windows
You plough through our dreams
You take away the ones we love
You disturb the peace

And when we really need you the
most

You never come

## Confession

I sit and wait
for something
to happen

When something
happens,
I hide until it
disappears

When it is gone,
I chase it
breathlessly

I catch up
to it
and drink the
last, sour
dregs

I sit and wait
for something
to happen.

### Lear Jet

three days awake
  a ghost of myself
    on the six o'clock
      train
        out of nowhere

in the Pelican sky;
  a Lear Jet navigates
    a perfect figure of eight
      vapour
        trail

I follow it
  round and round
    until my eyes
      are pinballs-

      'somebody up there likes me'

and the man
  directly opposite
    with the blue overalls
      and Jackboots

who muttered
  'I just ate my
    mothers head'

is just
  cheap MDMA,
    oozing from
      my scorched skin

**Delivery Truck**

Friday night
radio phone-in

static voices,
hushed

The girl on line one keeps
saying

    'I was just a child…
just a child.…I didn't mean to hurt
anyone'

Halfway to tears
    radio distortion
seasoning her voice
    with a strange electrical
sadness.

The host of the show
    offers some
      tenderness-

'Honey, I was a care child
    myself… it's hard coming out
of that system into the world…
    …it's easy to see how a fire lit
out of frustration can have tragic
consequences. What's important
is…'

They go on
like this

for an hour or more
back and forth
between
emotions,
all the while
the radio signal
becoming weak,
fading to white
noise
then re-appearing
at intervals of
conversation

We trundle
on
across County
borders,
past marshlands
and Moors,
Parish Churches
and faraway cities

This rattling
ribcage
of a truck
rolling through
the night
like some
prehistoric
hearse
ready to deliver
dinosaur bones
to the
wet earth

**East of the River**

East of the
river-

they found a
floating body
on a burnt-out bed

and a burnt-out Ford
in a dentist's
drive

and a dentist's drill
in a
horses hind

and a
horserace bookie
in a hooker's hind

and a
hooker hanging
from a
cathederal beam

and a
cathederal dean
in a
blackmail scandal

and a
blackmailedmother
on
regional news

and
regional anger
towards
a local detective

and a
detective's body
on a
burnt-out bed

floating East,

East of
the river

## The Game

Wet
black
darkness
lips
against
glass
tyre iron
swinging,
waiting
in the wet
grass.
Moisture
on your shoulder
click-jump
of the train
both of us
are ready
to take
the plunge
again.

## All this Land

all this land
passing
underneath
us

blue lakes
salt flats,
wheat fields,

cities alive
with lights
and
some
dead

not a soul
down there
knows of
love,

our love
at least

and that's all
that
matters
to me

## Sleep Movie

she wants to
audition
for one of my
sleep movies,
she tells me

I say jesus,
none of them ever
make it to
film
youknow

they just kind
of float around
my head
for most of the
night
then disappear
into
nothing

I don't care
she says

n' another thing

don't think
I'm not
good enough
for the role
because
I am,
I'll show you
I am

and she bursts
into floods
of tears,
slumped up against
the bus stop

I try to
console her

fix her hat

wipe mascara
tears
from her cheek
with my
thumb

OK I say
if you want
to be in
the scene
where

the girl's
at the bus stop
crying,
mascara tears
running
down
her cheek
an a huge
blue
Labrador
tongue

comes shooting
from
the sewer,
grips around
her ankles
an drags
her down
to that
red room
where theres me
and that
woman
who looks
like my
mother
in two thousand
years

and
Anthony Da
Costa
playing
a
huge
Hammond
Organ
on an
aquarium
coffin-

then that's
fine by me,
you passed
the audition

**I Wonder When...**

I'm reading
    'The Beach Of Falesa'

I'm reading
    'The Beach Of Falesa'

I'm reading a book
    by Dylan Thomas

I'm so excited I can't read

I wonder what's behind
    those trees?

Under that volcano?

In that kidney-shaped
    keepsafe?

I wonder when they'll let me
    back into the Isle
        of Man?

I'm reading
    'The Beach Of Falesa'

## Found in the Attic of 223 Millhouse Lane

Two
two-headed
boys
in front
of their
mother

one, a
master mariner,
two a
tailor of
fine silk
and linen
the other
a thief
of exotic
birdseggs and

rare tropical
beasts.

The four of
them;
eight-eyed,
two-bellied,
twenty-toed,
four-brained,
each
stand awkward,
dicky-bowed
before a
cameraman

halfmooning
with their
mouths

## Out to the Woods

out to the
woods,

staring out toward
the trees

trying to imagine

I'm trying to get nearer
to sleep,

catch the ghost.

But instead, I think
about meeting her again

and all those feelings
come surging back.

So I go over every possible
scenario-

prepare myself

dummy run every lie
I'd have to defend
in the morning,

spell them out
under my tongue
like the lines
to some
unfinished play,
left to burn
on a caravan site
bonfire

## The Chase

Police helicopter
tearing up
the sky
as if it were
tracing paper,
tearing through
the dark
with
silver teeth-
the wind
and the sea
and the narrow
winding
avenues,
and one phonecall
that sends
a hundred
toilets
hurriedly
flushing,
and blinking
living room lights
that
say

'run'

### Migration

migration

    from the silver earth

to the silver sky

    from the reeds and
the brooks,
eddy's hocking out
frantic geese at the
sound of a
    gunshot

'CLACKUUUUUUUUUUUM'

'quark quark quark quark
    PAPUM
      PAPUM
        PAPUM'

an inkwell explodes
    in the heavens

I watch all this
from the motorway
hard shoulder,
    in the backseat,
broken down

my father's car

hazardlighting
all over
the motorway.

Suddenly, an orange
Jacket through
the fog.

Muffled conversation
through the
whoosh of traffic.

I fall to sleep.

Half an
hour later, I wake
and
our own migration has
resumed

beyond
a line of trees on
the horizon,
I see the blinking
light of a skyscraper
spire

and imagine myself
crawling towards
it

## Double Helix

I can see a
double Helix

right in front of
my eyes; real enough
to touch

spinning and swirling
with the blueprint of all
life

and there's a girl
on the couch next to me

she's talking but I can't
really hear her

she says she wants to be
a Taxidermist I think

or an Alchemist

or an active chemist

or an axe-wielding activist

I can't decide

all I know is, she's talking at me

with no sign of letting up

best to keep looking forward
into the kitchen
where there're more
people

that way she'll think
I can't hear her

and maybe stop

all the while this illuminous
strand of DNA
dancing before my eyes
like a whirling dervish

everything smells
of Love Hearts
and
cough syrup

## Jane Cassidy

I knew her from school
every day she was dropped from
the sky
by a gliding stork
she was wrapped in a white
blanket
and by first bell
her cries had been humbled out
her tears had merged with the
blue rain
she crawled through those gates
made by Rhodesian lion hunters

I watched her from the grass
embankment
and laughed, and spat fourteen
yards

I didn't see her then
until a fire alarm spilled out
onto the gravel playing
fields
and someone had lit a big one
in the gauze bushes
and a girl cried pregnancy in a
labaratory
sirens rang out above plumes of
woodsmoke
Burning Burning Burning

I watched her skip into line
from a smashed window,
we'd made a domino trail from
cigarette ends
that sidewinded around the
windowledge like a Boa
Constrictor

she still looks cartoon, I thought,
and detonated

by lunch
she strode down the main corridor
and gritted her teeth like the
Matterhorn
the corridor where John met Jenny
and Teri met Vito
and Vito had a Bowie knife
pulled across his eyesocket.
All of them, everyone in fact,
moved out of the way
even the cock of year twelve
deferred

I heard about this in a canteen
queue
and believed it all a Chinese
whisper.

A bulldozer couldn't have done
that
I confided myself

by final bell
her dull golden hair was
surrounded by
red winged Garudas
that blocked out the sun,
a serpents pronged tail
jacknifed around her torso
grown men wept
as she blunderbussed out to
where the buses waited

I went out to face her,
sure of myself,
sure of her

and I laughed out the
side of my mouth
as I approached

bouncing over the cobbles,
hands pocketed

she incinerated me
then,
with a single
word.

## Jigsaw

everything in the
middle has been
forgotten

only the bright
beginnings
and slow,
blurred end
remain

all the other
details-

the slow silences
in the midnight
movie,
lying jigsawed
together

the hotel check-ins,
laughing up
fire escape stairs
to the seventh floor
room
and eventual

dressingown
theft

slicing tomatos
on rainyday
choppingboards
with no news
to speak of

catching eyes
in a wingmirror
and pretending
its a body
in the boot
we can both
hear banging

in a bakinghot taxi
through
town

it's these parts that
get covered in dust

forgotten

the middle parts

### Daisy

I rode on the back
of a bright white
cow

dappled
grotesquely
on its hide
in blood-red
were shapes-

snowflakes,
Africas,
shamrocks
and rivers of
dribbling lava.

She had a big
long
pink tongue
that lapped up
the loose
earth
on the ground
in front
of us,

every slurp echoing into
the long night.

We had been walking for
hours, and
somewhere along the
way, I felt a

presence tugging
at my dressing gown

it wanted to scare me,
whatever it was

but I was far too hungry
for fear

I licked my lips and caught
hold of its neck

it acquiesced into my belly
then disappeared
with a loud scream.

We passed a Farmhouse
with lots of people
outside in the dark

and someone was heard
to shout
from a big black-painted
barn

'one a them even wrote a whole
booka pomes. A whole books whorth
hehehehehehe!!!!'

A hay bale burst into flames.

There was a gazebo
in the distance,

with christmas lights
around the entrance,
riding the white
fabric in the wind

though nobody was
around, there were
great long tables
full of food.

We loped on,
towards it. Me
and my
ghost-

slowly, we
were
joined by fourteen
or fifteen more-
a herd!
A herd of
white cattle
and me

wandering to
a huge
deserted
banquet table
under the
sky
with our mouths
hanging open-

starving

## Friday Double Feature

Friday
Double Feature
at the cinema

Mally and Paul
duck the
turnstiles

and crawl into
the dark, haunted world
of screen
three

while Afternoon
turnstoevening
turnstonight

Paul on the
second-to back row,
feet up on the higher, more
tilted seats

Mally
sits two rows
from the front
and fills his empty

cup holder
full to the brim
with chocolate
peanuts

not a word
is said
for five and a half
hours

other nights
they would walk
the quarter mile
up the valley
road
to the cliff edge

sit quietly on
a limestone
outcrop,
tie a torch
to a piece of rope
and fish
for    falling

stars

### Masie

someone
   set a lake down
in front of me

an' surrounded it
   with big bushy
      Redwood trees

then poked their big
   finger into the blue
sheet of night
      and made a moon

all around me, gauze
   bushes, nettles, mulberry
bushes and molehills
     sprang up out of
the moist earth

the same someone
   set a pier down
     onto the lake

it went all the way out
   to the middle
where the moon licked
    its silver tongue across
      the tiny landing stage

I saw it then

moving

a single white Bull
walking toward me

it seemed to have
fire in its eyes,
its slow gait rocking
the pier from side
to side

as quickly as it appeared,
it burst into a gallop

the thing was enormous.

I was rooted to the spot
as its hooves touched
the ground

at that moment,
I vomited up
a .36 revolver
from my
throat

I held it there, in my hands

but I didn't know
how to load it

I didn't know
how to load it

## New Orleans, Seacombe Ferry

when the driftwood had dried on
the jetty
and Termites had turned into
hollow translucent lanterns
that had blown out
with the breeze

when on the roadside in town,
televisions and radios lay
melted in the harsh sun,
screens twisted,
grotesque branches of cooled
plastic oozing around
the grids
like lava

when
a holy man limped
up a pedestrianised
high street
dragging a swollen foot
behind him, tiny skulls
and sparrowbones dangling
from his hair
mumbling something to
himself,
almost chanting

it went something like
this-

'Holymarymotherofgodprayforus…........Badoum! Badoum!
Stfrancisxaviershakekalinda….…..........Badoum! Badoum!
Fathermichaelwasazombie….…............Badoum! Badoum!'

when in a projector room
at the school of
tropical medicine,
an Angolan fire snake
spewed out a pellet of
Zyklon B
and danced the limbo
under a
blackboard

when a dairy truck that
had impaled itself
on the highest branches
of a supermarket car park
tree
and started to smell
like decomposing flesh

and Albatross that circled
and Crows that shot from the sun
and things that sprang from the
thin air and looked for skin
to squirm beneath

found only mildew and mould and
no flesh at all

and moped away in search of
carrion,
dead postmen with their veins
strewn across the road by some
fleeing coastguard truck or
school bus

they could pick at them, if they
were still there

when the Christmas Eve window
display
had been turned into
makeshift barracks,
palisades of fake snow
bound together with tinsel
and the crackle of fairy lights
around peepholes

that made a movie set
of their surroundings

and a mans brain
surveying everything
from inside a hot water
bottle
as smooth and perfectly formed
as when it was lifted
from its skull

lying there, with nobody to claim it

when all this had happened
and nearly half a year
had passed-

thats when we wondered
if anyone was
ever really coming

## Gilroy Ponds

don't follow us down
here
they said

so we followed

turn back now
they said

so we tracked their footprints in
the dust

if I see you once more…..
they said

one of them was smoking

you don't want to look at this,
believe me

which worked us into a nervous
frenzy

so we climbed a tree

and followed their bright jackets
with our eyes

until they reached the river

and we saw it
face down, floating.
It was the colour of a bruised
banana

and them, pushing it out
with sticks

back out to the middle,
where it drifted in a circle

it would come back then, on
the slow current

like it was hungry

one of them hurled a rock, and it
flipped over on to
its front

and that's when we jumped down,
and ran
and wished to God
that we'd listened

**Multiplex**

a clear blue crystalline
light
surrounds the Multiplex
above the high empty vista
of sleeping department stores
and shoe shops,
elegant confectionary counters
with their shutters down,
clean chutes of wind
swooping in from the
docks
arranging
discarded receipts and empty
bags
into echoed snare rolls

pssssss tete psssss tete pssssssss

This light-

we're drawn toward it,
took a detour from
the night bus
to see it,
climbed huge steps
that were built last year
to resemble the entrance of
an Amphitheatre
a pink balustrade wedged
into plastic grass
framing the whole
thing.
We climbed all of this
to reach the holy summit

and stand there

and stare

and let our senses bathe in
the humid air

the faint lilt of caramel from
still-warm popcorn machines
dancing on the breeze

movie posters lit like Greek
statues,
Leonine caricatures,
frozen

the hum of electricity
underground

everything bright, clean,
spotless

we move toward the
globe lights
above the huge plate
window of the
Cinema
and press our faces
to the glass

we stand there for
a while,
watching

to see if anything
moves

### Um's n' Ah's

the heavens have
opened today

and we all know what
that means

we can all
start reading again

yr comics
yr atlas
yr readers digest
yr readers wives
yr smut
yr filth
yr holy texts
yr filth
yr boiler maintenance manual
yr Southern Gothic
yr Diary of a Madman
yr Finnegans Wake
yr Stax biography
yr brothers letter

yr mothers letter
yr cookery book
yr history of voodoo
yr Andalusia
yr Braille
yr court summons
yr ums n' ahs
yr lists

we can all
hide behind the couch
when the doorbell sounds

watch poplars drink up
the rain
from blurred windows

stare at the kettle while it boils

the possibilities are endless!

We all wanted that,
didn't we?

## Nothing Much to Write Home About

the night moved

the sea moved with it

some light had a hold of the water,
though it wasn't moonlight, the
moon was nowhere to be seen

it was a phosphorous light

almost electric

like the swirling neon that surrounds
power station cooling towers
on humid nights

blooms of Jellyfish moving with
the slow tide,
              basking in the illumination

we watched it for a while and heard
the whistle of a Herring Gull

the light intensified

Aja walked to the water, took out her
camera and tried to capture
its glow

but all she caught was a murky grey
nothing

some things, we decided, weren't
meant to be made
              into trophies

## Out of The Ballantyne

I walked
with dust
on my tongue

stray
cement
showered my
lightbulb
skeleton
spine

electrical
tape
over my
eyes

and nobody
came
to greet
me.

From
behind
boarded
up
baywindows
and
bolted
doors

I heard them:

a blood chant,

a passage from
the bible
being read
backwards,

stray dogs
squealing,

lads who
I'd played pool
with
in the Anchor
sawing
through floorboards-

muffled laughter.

I called out
for
Christie
but my voice
had long
since
run
for the last
bus

## The Tongue Professor

There was a man
who called himself
'The Tongue Professor'
who used to sit on
the platform
at Leasowe station
in just his breifs,
a pair of black
Wellingtons
and a Derby hat,
chainsmoking.

Whenever somebody
came into the station,
he'd flop over to em
and say something like-

"Now noner you people know, or could just as well
   envisage what it's like to touch heaven mmmmmm
   I can tell yers I touched it!I seen Hell too! Can't see
   one without the other unless all children take on the
   faces of Crows!"

(This would be spoken in an Old Testament
   American accent and have nothing to do
   with anything from the Bible)

One of his eyes
was big and
round,
and the other
was a slightly
discoloured, painted
pebble, which
was a pinkish hue

due to his
eyelid bleeding
when he wore it for a
couple of hours or
more. He used to
pop it out and show
it to people.
he called it his
'Cherry Blossom'

All of this is true.

My Uncle fixed
his generator
once,
out there on the farm
and the debt was
paid
with a hubcaps
worth of stuffed,
decorated birds.

The Tongue Professor
considered himself
an artist,
and believed his
works to be
legal tender, as
valuable as cash,
gold, silver, brass,
poultry or cattle.

Many other people
did too,
including my
Uncle

**Two Angels**

two angels in the front seat

feet pressed up against the
windscreen,
asleep on each others shoulders

and a driver
who hasn't spoken
a word since
he ran over a stray
Alsatian
on the way out
of the depot

the dull clunk
and a yelp

then teary-eyed, dragging
the mangled
corpse
behind a nursing home
skip,

entrails and intestines and

blue blood
glistening in the sun,
a Victorian operating
table
in the road

all that seems
a world away now,
as we plough on down this
highway

sheet lightning over a distant
valley

flashing lights on a hotel
lay-by

all of us, everyone passing through

dreaming through our
eyelids

none of us quite knowing where it
will end

**The View From The Back**

Cass read a book

        said he'd read it in one
        day

the book was 'The Old Man
and The Sea' by Ernest
Hemingway

        said it gave him new life,
new perspective

        off the back of it, he'd
written four songs this week
        already

and it was only Tuesday

I realised then, that we're all
in the same Cinema

        watching the same
        movie

You've just got to look for
some different seats every
once in a while

        they're everywhere,
        all around us

**Too Long**

too long, in books

too long, my own narrative

too long, head bowed

too long in one way conversation

pulling the ground apart

searching for the railtrack

some earthly rhythm at least

its momentum, is what it is

I think I'm seeking

a way to glide over this terrain

gain a distance, of sorts, between days

days that never cease

or change the colour of the marsh

or the colour of anything, for that matter-

everything's stayed the same since February

and I'm still brassic.

Flat on my back now,

pausing for a smoke-

the sky never seemed so big

**Exerpt**

She's piercing
her sisters ears
on the bed

sit still
she says
or I'll miss

then
Michael Brown's
a pervert
you know

and don't go
near the
new Melrose
flats

and
when we die
do we have
to move house
again?

don't be silly
when we die
we go to
heaven

that's where

mum says
dad lives

do we get to see
him when we
arrive?

inexorable
pit pat of
rain on
the roof

days running
into each
other
without
collision

time
cremated
under telegraph
wires

sit still
she says

just sit still!

or else
I'll miss
your ear

### Time in a Bottle

Brumal sun
retreating

epaulettes of
rain
on traffic wardens
shoulder

families huddled
under
umbrellas

businessmen
scurrying
to secret
multi-storey
trysts

we're gridlocked
here
on the dock
road

'It's like the cars are
needles
just weaving in and out
of each other

none of them ever
getting
any place'

I look at her and say

did you just make that up?

she laughs

I'm gonna use that!

are you?

yeah! in fact I'm gonna use this
bit too

what, all of it?

yeah, all of it

## Wake-up call

to look at him
you'd think

he's really caught
the muse

he's talking non-
stop

he's excited

he can recognise love and
hate and can
accept them both,
free of doubt

right now-

he's supping his first
Guinness

say's he's written
this song
and wants me to play some
piano on it

like a Tim Hardin feel

I say I'd love to

this bug he's got,
its infectious

I wouldn't mind a dose
of it myself…..

time to get poor
again
burn some utility bills
get drunk and build a fire pit
in the yard

get irresponsible

-time to get my act together

**Blimp**

There're lots of people
here
who she knows
and who she used to
know

there's a man
talking through
a broken
microphone

music,
rides,
a Chair-o-plane
and a fierce sun

all these faces
coming at her
some of them blurred,
strange faces

some familiar,
aged faces
that don't appear
real
somehow

further away,
there's an anchored
balloon
in the shape of a
vaulting horse
on a tight wire
floating high above
the sea

it's this that's grabbed her
attention for some reason

she can't seem to take
her eyes off it

## Taxi Cab

Taxi cab taxi cab
run me home
run me out of this town
with a burning branch
at my neck

run me till the
balls of my
feet are blistered
and fat Rottweiler-headed
women
laugh at me
from pink limousines
at the mouth
of the tunnel

carry me
across the water
to where I belong
with the open fields,
the brick factories,
the all night sunbeds,
the clairvoyant
florists,
the foster families with
huge four by fours
and
tall Christmas trees

standing openarmed
at picketfences,
grinning out of their
gums

send me back to the sticks
where glass
pyramids
stand tall over the
horizon
and four-day mullets
wear droplets of
liquid sunshine
like
tiny pearls

and petshops send midnight
search parties out
for escaped
Anacondas

every one
of the above
will welcome me back
as one of their
own

if you'll only stop
for me
taxi cab

on this endless road
in the new rain

if just one of you
will stop

**Brother**

Brother, I see you

I see you over that red river

standing there, frozen

your iron ribcage silhouetted
against the moon

everything covered,
your spine, your brow, your gilded
fingernails, your webbed feet and petrified
joints

your cracked mouth and broken arms
still open,
still poised to receive

all of you covered in rust the colour
of blood

do you know we're still here, brother?

we have been for a long time,
long before you went to sleep

and left us cowering in your dull
shadow

that never moves with the passing
of the sun